AN ARM FIXED TO A WING

AN ARM FIXED TO A WING
POEMS
OLIVIA CLARE FIEDMAN

LOUISIANA STATE UNIVERSITY PRESS   BATON ROUGE

Published by Louisiana State University Press
lsupress.org

Copyright © 2025 by Olivia Clare Friedman
All rights reserved. Except in the case of brief quotations used in articles or reviews, no part of this publication may be reproduced or transmitted in any format or by any means without written permission of Louisiana State University Press.

LSU Press Paperback Original

Designer: Kaelin Chappell Broaddus
Typefaces: Fournier, text; Acumin Pro, display

Cover illustration: *Fish Magic*, 1925, by Paul Klee. Philadelphia Museum of Art, The Louise and Walter Arensberg Collection, 1950, 1950-134-112.

Library of Congress Cataloging-in-Publication Data

Names: Clare, Olivia, 1982– author.
Title: An arm fixed to a wing : poems / Olivia Clare Friedman.
Description: Baton Rouge : Louisiana State University Press, 2025.
Identifiers: LCCN 2024048596 (print) | LCCN 2024048597 (ebook) | ISBN 978-0-8071-8373-1 (paperback) | ISBN 978-0-8071-8436-3 (epub) | ISBN 978-0-8071-8437-0 (pdf)
Subjects: LCGFT: Poetry.
Classification: LCC PS3603.L3543 A88 2025 (print) | LCC PS3603.L3543 (ebook) | DDC 811/.6—dc23/eng/20241015
LC record available at https://lccn.loc.gov/2024048596
LC ebook record available at https://lccn.loc.gov/2024048597

*for Willa and Colin
and for Craig*

CONTENTS

ACKNOWLEDGMENTS *ix*

I.
Making Your Milk and Reading Valéry *3*
Before *4*
And Then for Daphne *5*
Sleeping *6*
Katherine *7*
Embracing Cities *8*
Dream of the Valley *9*
Elegy *10*
Four Months Old *11*
Not the Highest *12*

II.
CAMERA
POEMS
The Director *15*
Lankershim *16*
The Well *17*
Nobody *18*
She Looks Into *19*
After Lunch *20*
Blind Mink *21*
Camera, Gone *22*

III.
Finding Him *25*
Elegy for This Room *26*
Friends and Strangers *27*
The Age of Reproduction *28*
The Tenor Hours *29*

vii

Elegy for Gone Sounds *30*
Up *31*
Tuesday's Train *32*

IV.
I Asked Him *35*
Vow *36*
His Little Dream *37*
Wanda *38*
Meals *40*
Two Brothers I Knew *41*
Eating Alone *42*
Winter *43*
Christmas Eve *44*

V.
Reading about Florence *47*
When My Reverence Is Idle, I Stand Stunned *48*
Your Name *49*
Second Silence *50*
I Build a Machine *55*
Stradivarius *56*
Elegy for Your Contrition *57*
Weeks *58*
Mother *59*
Her Own *60*

ACKNOWLEDGMENTS

My thanks to the editors of the following publications in which the poems listed, or parts thereof, first appeared, sometimes in different forms or under different titles:

The Atlantic: "Before"; *Bat City Review:* "When My Reverence Is Idle, I Stand Stunned"; *Colorado Review:* "Sleeping"; *Denver Quarterly:* "Dream of the Valley"; *FIELD:* "Stradivarius"; *MARY:* "I Build a Machine" and "Weeks"; *Paris-American:* "Second Silence"; *Southern Review:* "Embracing Cities" and "Finding Him."

I am grateful to—

James W. Long and everyone at Louisiana State University Press;

MacDowell, Vermont Studio Center, Djerassi, Tin House, Black Mountain Institute, Iowa Writers' Workshop, the Olive B. O'Connor Fellowship at Colgate University, and the Rona Jaffe Foundation;

Ava Leavell Haymon, Jin Auh, Abram Scharf, Jessica Faust, Faith Hill, Stephanie G'Schwind, Brandon Krieg, Colleen O'Brien, Michael Rutherglen, Lee Pinkas, Maegan Poland, Lorinda Toledo, Ernie Wang, Joe Milan Jr., Becky Robison, M. O. Walsh, Rachel Hochhauser, Amy Silverberg, Ruth Madievsky, Ramzi Fawaz, Allegra Pedretti, Kathleen Bogart, Leah Breen Houk, Emily Nemens, Andrew S. Nicholson, Mary Belle Kirtland, and Mira Dalju;

my colleagues at the Center for Writers at the University of Southern Mississippi: D. M. Aderibigbe, Angela Ball, J. A. Bernstein, Adam Clay, and Monika Gehlawat;

Marianne Chan, who read early versions of these poems;

Donald Revell, Claudia Keelan, Mark Irwin, Janet Fitch, Mark Richard, and Emily Setina;

Marjorie, David, and Owen;

Petula;

and my father, Tibi.

This book is dedicated to Craig, Colin, and Willa.

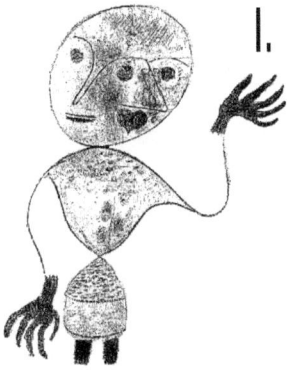

MAKING YOUR MILK AND READING VALÉRY

on the last time he saw Mallarmé,
who died soon after.
The book is balanced on my knees
and this machine's hooked
to my breasts with plastic tubing
impossibly hard to clean,
my body in the act of translating
all I've eaten and drunk to give
to you, mysteriously—and not so mysterious,
to those who understand it—
which is how I often choose to live,
allowing mystery when I know
explanations exist; that is,
they do, almost always. It's July 1898
and they are picking flowers in Valvins,
far from us in 2020, and not so far—
when you are older we will walk
with your father in simple flowers,
and speak as honestly as we can
of what language does and does not allow.

BEFORE

You remember this, don't you?
We said, later, we'd remember,
and now it's later. Do you?

You wrote your brother, then alive,
a long email (back when you wrote
and read for hours, we both did), and we slept

till eleven (back when we slept so late),
and if I don't write this down, it will
all fall away, but even I can't remember

which city that was, which bus we'd taken,
what we'd drunk the night before.
We'd been trying to save money,

we didn't eat, but we drank, and that
1:00 a.m. bartender gave us free rounds,
while we sang, not sure what

(knowing you, it was Italian), and we
drank, not sure what, because why,
it was free, our cups full, and then not,

and all we could do was walk back
how we'd come, stumbling toward
our anonymous room.

AND THEN FOR DAPHNE

You think yourself happy,
in Mediterranean clarity, leaned
to water. Knocked over
beach chair, hotel's playing cards
stacked in solitaire, all the gods

you're naming, the story
of nymph turned to tree you recite,
leaning eastward. Beast, beast,
beast to the sea. To the tree—
in my head all I hear
are sounds of her turning.

SLEEPING

I am not. You are not. He is not.
They told me this would happen,
at this age. They told us, before you
were born, *sleep while you can.*
I tried to avoid most people.
I was already being asked things
that were no one's business,
being told things I never asked
to be told. *Go to the movies, just you two.*
Go to dinner. And sleep, sleep now,
while you can. It was always that dramatic.
As if sleep is something to store,
an account we can, anytime,
draw from. Truth is, when I
do sleep, dreams are vivid now—
with me tunneling through,
and sometimes, within them,
there's you—and when I'm awake,
the ink of them, clouding everything.

KATHERINE

You look down as you talk.
The tablecloth has crumbs
from our meal. We've drunk
the whole bottle. I haven't seen you
in twenty years. Even in this world,
frighteningly connected,
we've lost touch. Your mother
is not well. Your father, all the time,
is at home, which for him,
is unusual. He used to
run marathons, he used to travel
to several countries as a doctor.
About your husband, well, you are
thinking of divorce. You don't
say it casually. I don't offer advice. I've been
married a few years. We both have
young daughters. We bring out our
phones, scroll through pictures.
One day, I say, they could meet.
Maybe soon, next week. I let myself
get excited, I realize I want friendship—
yours, something old becoming new.
In school, you were popular. Homecoming
court, captain of volleyball. In the halls,
you wore white jeans and Maybelline.
Who was I? Someone on the side.
So, I say again, maybe next week.
We'll see, you say. You pause,
sigh suddenly. Let's be honest, you say,
life's a bitch. I don't know
about that, I say. There are
better things to come, maybe
waiting for you. Oh, you say,
you're one of those types. You
look up, you sound betrayed. You're
one of those, you say. Of course.

EMBRACING CITIES

Now that I've known you
where I was born. I try
you. Here, they speak impossible
to you. I've said the ones
approximating happiness
I could speak to you—
preparing horses for the races,
into the horses' ears
their feral canter
the sorrel intervals
latent in desire
of forms and chaos

so long, I reenter the city
to understand
words, words I can't say
I remember, I've tried
in my sleep. Here,
they stand on boxes,
squaring verses on velocity
before the horses start
in four lines,
of verses
if desire is a city
at rest in us, *where?*

DREAM OF THE VALLEY

Once there was a valley of children
who would not speak, guarded
by children who would not speak.

The bronze Muse, anonymous gift,
to them was ornamental, an archaic
fountain. Children went to her

with copper wishes and attempted prayer.
Some heard her in their sleep and woke
and would not speak. A boy arrived.

He'd left his country to be near her.
He made noisy machines of teeth
and bronze tongues in the valley

and the children watched
and the children who watched
the children watched.

Now, his machines
are broken down. Ask
the children which way is out,

they point in all directions.

ELEGY

I am always saying your name.

It's 2023. I still don't understand the idea.
Not here. Death
and gone. I'll never.

What am I looking for?
A murmur of you. A wrinkle, a strand.
How to go back
to that life, with you in it,
a firm yolk inside,
not escaping.
I'll never

be used to this—*without you.*
May I never.
May I never be used to
the days keeping on

as if *without you*
was all I knew.

FOUR MONTHS OLD

Our dreams are so vivid, we both say,
every time we wake up,
which might be 2:00 a.m. or 6:00 or 10:00,
waking up with her, helpless,
ready to suck, ready to eat.

Are you dreaming about her yet?
I ask my husband. My own dreams
haven't caught up with
the present. They—the dreams—
think it's ten years ago,

or two, or sometimes more,
and I am four or five, in my
childhood room. I don't know
how to tell them. *Dreams,
wake up. Dreams, you are here.
Right now. This year. I am married.*

I've had a baby. Understand.
But they keep on,
bringing me back, further
in memory than I've ever gone,
and in some, I'm helpless,
and in some, I've no idea what
age this is.

NOT THE HIGHEST

A friend tells me there are levels to heaven.
I can't bring myself to believe her.
Her father told her this,
that her own dead mother

lives in one of the levels, not
the lowest, not
the highest, somewhere
in between. "So purgatory?" I say.

No, something different, because
this is heaven. Within heaven
are these levels. "Don't worry for your mother,"

her father told her. "She has everything
she needs." We're in the car at night,
while my friend tells me this. We're about to

say goodbye for, we know, a long time.
"He said she has 'everything,'" she said.

"But no. 'Everything she needs'
is not everything."

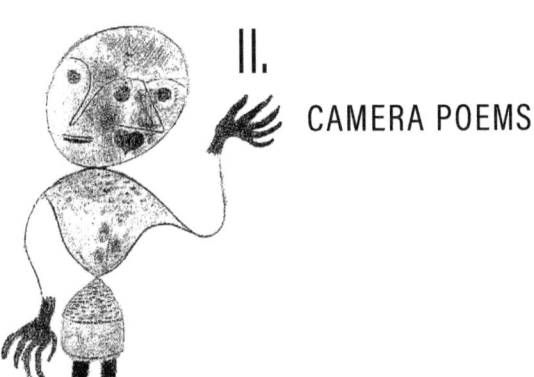

II.
CAMERA POEMS

THE DIRECTOR

"Pay attention," the Director said. "Look at me."
He waited for her to look at him. He said:
"Do you realize what a shit take that was?"
"It was?" she said.
"Pure shit," he said. "Not even," he said,
"as good as mucus on shit. Mucus on top of shit
smells better than that."
She hid her mouth with her hand.
"I'm not laughing," he said. "Do you see
me laughing?"
"I'm sorry," she said. "It's just that
sometimes I smile when I don't know
what else to do."
The Director blinked, his eyelids
corn-husk rough, his eyes themselves
the color of corn. He'd had seven wives
in his lifetime. Everyone knew it.
Then he said, "Are you—are you really
even aware of the camera?"
"Absolutely," she said.

She looked up at it then—
that one-eyed beast,
that whirring fiend,
that mammoth king,
gliding along its tracks.

LANKERSHIM

She's being watched from all sides.
No, this is how it *feels*, that she's
being watched. Is anyone even
looking at her? She's on the bus,
back from the shoot, makeup still on,

her hair greased back, lipstick hardened,
and the palm trees moving silent,
like a film unspooling, rare LA rain
freckling the window. No, nobody

is watching her. That man over there
is asleep, his arms crossed, his head
drooping down, and this woman's
on her phone, and that man's
on his phone, and that woman is too,
and that one, and that man to her right
           is praying the rosary,

she sees the beads in his hand,
the cross trapped in the man's fist,
and if he ever looks back, looks
to her, she'll look at him too,
as if with a shared thought,
and that will be something true,
almost something to touch, she thinks,

    there, there,
but maybe his eyes are closed,
she can't see his eyes, *that's
the trouble,* and then the bus skids,
and the bus dips back.

THE WELL

She is giving things she doesn't have.
That's what the Director tells her. "Don't piss
in the pot," he says. "If you don't have the real thing,
don't piss in there. It has to be in you already."

"Say the line again," he tells her. She looks down
for a beat, collects something within herself,
looks to him with heat
pumping through her, she hopes.

"Don't talk to me like that," she says.
"Don't you ever talk to me like that."
She waits. He waits. "Okay, okay, good," he says.
"Now, again, and this time, gather it,

let it course through you, do you know
what I mean?" She tells him she does.
She looks down for a moment, collects
something in herself, looks back up.

"Don't talk to me like that," she says.
"Don't you ever talk to me like that."
"Good," he says, "now louder."
"Don't you ever talk to me like that!"

"Good, good, now this time, okay,
contain it. It's coursing, but you're holding,
holding. When you speak, let it go. Got it?
When you say the line, release it."

She looks down, she collects, she waits.
He waits. She makes him wait
a little longer. "Say it again," he says.
"Again." And she makes him wait,

makes him, more, and then
longer, a little longer.

NOBODY

The trouble is—first, everyone
is watching her. The Director, all crew,
the makeup artist knitting a shawl
just behind the camera
as her weeping scene goes on.
Blessed, blasted camera.
Then the trouble is—camera off,

nobody's watching. *I am a nobody.*
Stop, don't think it. You have your mother,
your sister. You mean something.
She starts to call Anna, her sister
in Tampa—pharmaceutical sales,
three children—because it is something
worthwhile to hear someone's voice,
remarking, *aah*ing, loving. Anna

was always in awe—Hollywood,
dressing rooms, all of that. But it's been
a while, a long while. It's too hard
to dial the number. Best just let it be.
Last time, at least, they could say
"love you" in the end—but this time,
if she waited for it, and if it did not come,
she would feel her own innards
ripped. That was the line last time
from Anna—*Joanie, I love you*—
simple, quaint,
she'd hold on to. Anyway,
that was awe enough.

SHE LOOKS INTO

Her mirror,
her own muggy bathroom,

lets her eyes soften and blur, her vision fog—
there, her image is split

into angles, into radiating parts.

    She is splintered

to selves,   not broken, harmonious,
all existing at once,
so that if she were to   speak the name
of each one, each self   she could name
herself   at once.

AFTER LUNCH

She says to the Director,
"Where do you want me?"
New scene. He won't tell her what he wants.
The camera is rolling.
"Can I move around?"
"Yes, move," he says.

She moves to a chair. Doesn't sit in it but stands behind,
puts her hands on it.
"Now what?" she says.
"Just talk to me," he says.   "And say what?" she says.
"Tell me where you're from."   "But that's not the character."
"Look straight into the camera." "But that's not—"
"Don't worry about that.
"Tell us something, tell us
who you are."

She has never done this with the camera rolling.
                              "My name is Joan," she says.
                              "My sister calls me Joanie. I'm from
                              Tuscaloosa."
"Just stand there," says the Director.
"Be you. Try to be you."

She has never done this—the camera on—
in all her life. She stands. She *is*.
No one says anything. The crew, a dozen of them,
are silent. The Director coughs. Quick.
He goes back to not coughing, to listening,
to watching. A warmth sweeps from her feet,
travels all the way up to her face, releases itself
through her eyes. She is crying. *Oh God*. She thinks
she could do this a very long time.

BLIND MINK

She is waving her hand in the air.
She is talking, saying the same lines
again and again, in her dark closet
with the door closed, the closet like a deep hull,
inside the inside, because this is where
she begins to understand the language of what
she is saying, each syllable. This is what
a teacher once told her. *Think only
of what you're saying. Act on the lines,
not between.* She is forcing herself
to think only the monologue's words,
their meaning, even though this
is her hundredth time, repeating.
Then she ends, she stops.
*Make your mind blank. Blank mind.
Blank mind.* She has her own mantra
to help her end, to find a vastness,
an inner clearing. *Blank mind. Blind mink.
Ink lid. Kid link. Mid-blink.*
Now she'll sit a long time, silent,
she won't even open the door.
This is how the words
empty, her mind goes bare, and then
she imagines: a great storm, leaves gather,
plume, the trees knock
against themselves, falling over,
disappearing, all the roots
in the earth, the ground moving,
the roads rolling like carpets,
vanishing, and the sky, too, vanishing.

CAMERA, GONE

As she is dialing, she thinks—
*Think only of what you're
saying. Not how it sounds.
Only what you mean. Nothing but that.*

It's ringing. Her curtains are closed.
Outside, she knows, the sun
is almost a nub.
All this Los Angeles glow
becoming twilight, and here she is—
calling her sister, asking herself
to expect nothing, but wanting something,

because of course she wants,
and she wants to want,
and just after the fourth ring—
Anna's voice, her actual voice, answering,
and—maybe?—wanting too,
and Joan says, "Hi there, it's been a long time,"
and Anna agrees, and Anna laughs,
and Joan does too, and, while they talk,
Joan opens the curtains, because
the end of the day is giving her
a trail of pink, a touch of violet.

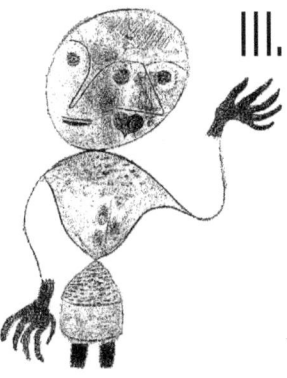

FINDING HIM

When the heart gives out
you must use your whole body
to bring it back. That's what
my husband tells me,
who's begun doing this

for a living. It takes two people,
switching off, counting
chest compressions to the beat of
the Bee Gees, if it helps. Bringing back
a heartbeat takes the whole self,
two selves, sometimes

many. There was the story of
the little boy who fell
in the forest. They found him
that way, among the crisscrossing oaks,

all the living things scurrying
around him. He'd been there
for some time, having

walked out the front door entirely
on his own. They did compressions
for a long while. Paramedics breathed
into his airway. We have deep wells
within us, I'm convinced. During this,

it is believed, the child's heart
restarted three times. He
came back to life again, again,
and again. I will end
the story there.

ELEGY FOR THIS ROOM

                                        It's a curse
to love things as you leave them—we're packing
this shelf of our collected Woolf and Freud,
Morrison and Wilde, discarding postcards,
ancient checkbooks, electric bills,
and leaving the cat's missing tooth

lost somewhere in this room. I've done it
so many times, woken up not knowing
where we are quite, where's this, what now, how here,
        now this, says the local news, every place
we go, and how this one ends, friends, we do not know.
                That's the trouble: we've got no answers, though
we've asked, and beyond that, I've looked
in the carpet, the cat's water bowl, near
everywhere, for that chipped fang.

FRIENDS AND STRANGERS

Over and over, I dream the same spaces.
The same houses I used to know.
In this house with the sorrowing tree
in the front, a magnolia
pregnant with scent,
there was a neighbor's rose garden
on the other side of my bedroom.
And in this one, a late relative's house,

there's the room I slept in,
the four-poster bed, the curtainless window
looking out to the town's
one drawn road. Sometimes in the dreams
in the room—my room—
there are people I don't know,
talking or waiting, I don't know
what for, and anyway, what

are they doing here, waiting
in a room that isn't theirs?
Acting as though they have
nowhere to go, all of them people
I know from different cities, various
times, and they don't even sit, they just
stand and talk,
some of their faces distinct, others
blurred, and here I am, in my own bed,
trying to sleep, and there they are,
their gossip, they must think
they've got
all night.

THE AGE OF REPRODUCTION

I sat on a bench by the river
and tried to write a history.

A lamentation of women
in red hats fed crumbs
to reflections of swans.
No one stepped within
five feet of the water.

I can't remember the last baptism,
said a red hat. None of us come
near what we've heard is holy.

She took off a high heel.
She traced a ripple with her toe
and made what some would call
the image of a lady.

THE TENOR HOURS

These fevered voices gather,
I bleed songs—emptied swings rapt

in breeze, their fixed creed
replays without my own

knowing it. Motion, I am sick,
a plunderer in sun who

can't conclude from color or light
rain closing in. Some songs

I keep all night
in tenor hours,

I keep my harrowers.

ELEGY FOR GONE SOUNDS

Turn off all music. If I can't have
sounds I remember—my father
coming home, the arriving
engine, a midnight door

opening—
I want nothing new.
Nothing soothes.
It gets like that.
Leave me.

Over the days,
I am smaller,
remembering less.
No one can see
what little of me
there is.

I'm staying still. Alone. No one
even talk.

This is the way of things
until I imagine
something else. Grass
beneath me. Something breathes.

The first few notes
of a tune begin, anonymous
atoms. From where?
Me, possibly. I imagine

I am walking to rich ground.
I am walking to the center
of my own ear.

UP

I walk a road where each raindrop, a grace note,
runs the orange-scarlet stem
to the tips of these
diamond-pointed, downward
leaves. I walk a road of shaking

staccato, swaying, still
trees bowing a little, clouds
corresponding to none of these, and I'm led
to a man, not singing, writing, a flower
fastened to his pen, but how do I
speak, how to ask him
if his romanticism is
self-conscious and/or bold, ask him
to walk me back up
the Eurydicean road—if I
speak, nothing answers; if he
looks at me, I've left.

TUESDAY'S TRAIN

As she rode toward the west of America,
she saw, in the syntax of trees going by,
the landscape as time-lapse photography.

A chrysanthemum opened robotically,
and she thought, She won't be held here humanly.
She hunts no sense. Anonymous symbols, geometries,
patterning facts and ideas inherent among
tonotopically varying shades of sky
crossing indistinctly, vaulted neuroweathers,
a temple ceiling's latticework
of sodium, potassium, a painting
either by an ancient or future sect.
She counts no facts. Bees prismatically trapped
in oil.   Her life,
          a supernumerary cloud opens
into time-lapsed clouds above time-lapsed
statues, shuttle pads, glyphs, glens,
ceilings of the Louvre that don't move.

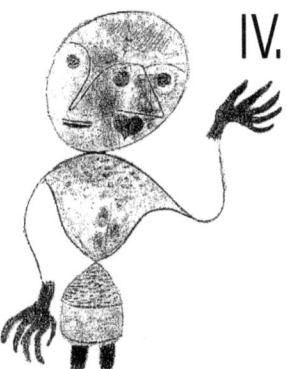

IV.

I ASKED HIM

About his religion.
He said, It's something
that one person can't say to the other.

It can't be broken into parts.
Think of a harp
for which there are too many strings.
An electric harp,
rhapsodizing in Orpheus's dream.
Think of the numb feeling
in your fingertips, when a harp's
numberless strings
have been plucked.

VOW

Coated in white film,
slight, downy head,
lips sucking in　　　　　　dear breath—
the first breath of all,
born here, born now,
fresh as an eye, on the earth's verge—
I will always, I will never—
but who am I, earth-worn,
in the midst of you?

HIS LITTLE DREAM

Be you animal or winged,
come no nearer; be you
lion or fox come to
croon or yowl or offer
your reflection,
be still! You flicker, you fume,
a patina of bronze
in his unlit room.

    He threw his blanket
and his stuffed, eyeless hound, then the sound
of faux fur on the floor, then the slow
and chalky outline of a cloud,
away, leave him be,
then one sound,
then nothing more.

WANDA

We sat on a satin sofa.
Between us: a disembodied, life-sized pair
of crossed plastic legs.

We were at Wanda's place.
A coat lay across her arms like a human body.
She was a collector of clothes and objects.

"I've got three more upstairs," she said.
"The woman in 4C died.
Her husband sold me this. World travelers.

He told me their boat was called *The World*.
So they'd sail the world in *The World*,
and step off *The World* and onto the world."

Wanda sold things out of her condominium—
three floors and a garage filled with used,
rare furniture, clothing, paraphernalia—
a stale-smelling, stuffed ark of endangered objects.

A rack of petticoats and bustiers,
a Viennese harpsichord,
mechanical dolls in their boxes,
figurines of cats holding parasols,

a table crammed with wood and glass Nativity scenes,
a mannequin dressed as an aviator.
In my own apartment, I had almost nothing.
A cat, a couch. Loans and debt.

I reached over. I tried to uncross the mannequin's
plastic legs. They wouldn't come apart.

"I could tell you about the end," Wanda said.

Once again, she was talking about the world.

"Don't," I said.

"It's like saying what happens at the end of a book," she said.

"You're really one of those people?" I said.

"It starts with an earthquake," she said.

She was standing on the other side of the room, but all she wanted was to tell me this.

"Interested?" she said.
I told her I wasn't.

"Sorry," she said. "I get going on a thing, and I don't stop."

Now she was crying quietly.
I looked away.

I grabbed the plastic legs. I smashed them across my knee and let the pieces fall to the floor.

MEALS

He'd been making breakfast every morning, always the same—toast, sausage, eggs. We'd done this so many days in a row. Those meals, our life,

a routine before the day started. Eat breakfast, exchange stories.

"Did I tell you about the time I went camping and broke my tooth?"
Yes.

"Did I tell you what happened that summer I worked at the city pool, and a little girl fell in the deep end?"
Yes.

On the day we began to repeat ourselves, I thought we were close to finished.
On the day we began to repeat ourselves, we'd only just started again.

TWO BROTHERS I KNEW

One of them, born with
an ocean in his mouth.

The other, his twin,
born lithe and long, loving almost
any woman he saw.   Out there—

his saddleheart, always riding,
searching the blue
for some kinship, or at least
a crimson-haired girl drinking
rooks from a glass.

EATING ALONE

I had a menu, ice water, a plate of sliced lemon. It was Friday, early, I was at the bar. Behind it, a man wearing wet gloves pulled his knife through an oyster. Next to me, a woman was on her phone, talking quietly. About the time she fell off a horse.
                    No, it wasn't awful, she said. She'd do it all again.
              She'd get on the horse, let herself be thrown. Rising, face up. Her legs cutting the air.
              The uncertainty, everything, the exhilaration.

WINTER

One year, you told me,
you were camping in the cold
and ran out of food.
You chewed a hard candle
like gum because you were
so hungry. You lost track
of the days. You lost your
watch and your way.
You started to think,
We're born into the world,
but why *this* one? There could
have been five suns, or leafless trees,
or none of that at all.
It wasn't so profound, you said,
but it was clear.
You realized you were talking
to yourself out loud, or else
you were talking
to a hundred
watchful souls.

CHRISTMAS EVE

On the bus ride home,
stars looked liquid.
Trees bowed down.
Memories gummed my brain.
The time I'd been too reasonable
about love. The unreasonable
time too. The time
I saw maggots eating a frog.
All of it ran together.
I was rum-drunk and cold.
I hugged myself for warmth.
My grandmother had raised me
in the home she still lived in.
I barely saw her.
In my forty years, I was
in love only once, and even that
was too much.
On the bus, a few others
were asleep, or deep in their phones.
      Three seats ahead, to my left,
a woman was swathed in a puffer coat.
A fleecy hood encircled her head.
She was my age, maybe a little younger.
In and out of sleep. Her eyes
would close, and when the bus
rocked, her eyes would open.
Her lashes were so long,
I thought, if I sat closer,
I might hear the pulse
of each blink. She had a face
that looked like she could
understand. I wanted
to sit beside her. I wanted
to tell her a few things
for which I hoped
to be forgiven.

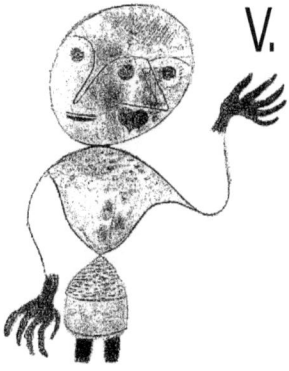

READING ABOUT FLORENCE

I am not in Florence. In fact,
not anywhere near. Years ago, I was.
Now, I'm at home—a chipped dish of yogurt,
my child sleeping in the next room,
this book in my lap, a book about
both beauty and ugliness.
The neighbor's dog is incessant.
I pretend the barks are music. I read
to their rhythm, in my dusky room,
about a day in the life, about
both beauty and disaster.

WHEN MY REVERENCE IS IDLE, I STAND STUNNED

An hour to watch the river—holy,
they say. On the bridge, men
talk and they don't look down.
Three boys steer a sculpture
      in a cart: an arm
fixed to a wing. One town
to share the ghost of God
with vigilant men who lay
the wing out to dry, clumsy
      in their gloves. Back
to my book: glass boats take marble
Gabriels to walled cities.
Men stand still. They're hungry
for religion, and the boats don't sink.
      I close the book
to count people I have loved,
approximating.

YOUR NAME

There's your voice again,
spilling in the dark.
Who am I to you? Somebody?
On Monday, I first heard you.
On Tuesday, you were there.
Wednesday, though, and
where are you? I even talked aloud,
trying to find you, asked
for you again. Thursday,
I was still looking, listening
in the spaces between minutes.
On Friday, in the morning,
your voice came, a whole minute,
and on Saturday, in the dark,
you were there. It was Sunday when
there was singing, like
thrumming, like rain clearing
caked dust, water running through
my brain, opening a channel,
tunneling clean making way.

SECOND SILENCE

i.

O what a pretty mouth
in the photo I've known you

had or had not seen what I could
Not seen what you are

I want to see a long
time My eyes like eyes
of a crow splayed wide
as my hand in the shadow of a tree's

red leaves and all
others green
I'd name the branches

of Yggdrasil Until there's no
more to be named

ii.

I go from this room
changing each thing changed

all this matter mattering
I trace you less

on the bed before you leave
like the Corinthian Maid
tracing the silhouette
of her shepherd on the wall

asleep against it the night
before he leaves
to war or Rome

iii.

I would have I would have
had him   *I would have her*

leave She the maid
starts her shepherd on the wall
head first an ear crossed out
All this accumulation All

this his profile in
parts I part I Rome

iv.

These sounds
coming through
from another place
like distant brasses

Beneath this
a floor holding me up
falls inward
Any irreal sound

terrible but the silence after
before fertile
And that second silence
shifts Gives way

v.

You in the room
a second self or near invisibility
from a story I've invented
but did not and did not want
to believe in

Your face
little stamp of late shadow
centered on your eye

Two notes fire from my head
Athena Athena
I can hold them
a swift dotted gash along
the blankness

The eye and ear collide
one sense organ of seeing-hearing

blue to thunder
beebuzz to blue

No paper
Noise of wheels against noiselessness

A hand struck through the thought
talking not with words
between fingers gaps between
sounds within the gaps Sounds

I BUILD A MACHINE

I build a machine like a jaw,
holes strung through from top to bottom
with catgut strings.

The machine records a man's
talk. I build teeth
inside the machine's jaw

and they pluck the strings,
each tooth a calcium plectrum
plucking the man's talk

better than the man.
Better than the man, the machine
tunes its own strings.

The sound of the jaw of the machine
opening is the sound
of a machine shutting down.

The sound of the jaw of the machine
opening is the sound
of a man waking up.

STRADIVARIUS

For the last time, not knowing
it is, she sight-reads the dead
man's sonata,

hearing in each note the
opposite silence—the yank
of her bow

from the A string. Most days
she won't think of the music
or suffer

its absence, a small death
when one doesn't remember
to remember

an absent thing. She won't
speak of the music and will
commemorate it

when she doesn't remember it—when
she hears a minor chord in the sound
of talk

from the next room and takes her
son on her lap and repeats to him
a word

she has always loved, though
she can't remember where
she read it.

ELEGY FOR YOUR CONTRITION

No one knows this house as you do.
Its puckered brick, flowers
pricking through the driveway's
fractured concrete.

Turning away—no one makes you.
Only you can do that.

The shame would be to let *turning away*
mean nothing,
let the place slip
through zones of memory,
down bottomless hulls.

Should that ever happen—
let it be your own trouble.
Let it be your great guilt
to confess.

WEEKS

Redundant cars, headlights.
Inside—the clock chant,
the lamplight.

Seven-spoke days
spinning in place
in snow. In the bedroom

chime the freezing pipes.
An audience of moths
flutters in ash,

shadows and shadows' snuff.
Two people

tumble in flurries of
goose down.

MOTHER

When her daughter was older,
she recited to her the names
of pigments, gems, and scents.
And she'd wear these
if she had them,
either on the shined
and penciled lines of her lids,
or in her ears as drops,
or in the folds of her clavicle,
                so her daughter
might smell myrrh cream
or phthalo clove. Might smell
(what she'd said could be) a huntsman's
rosemary, fabled
to give long life.
                Bedtime, and she played
a fretted electric instrument with strings
from a sheep's gut
and sang thinly, it seemed, on
a hair's breadth.
And she taught her daughter
the names of roots and made her cite
the precise color
of the eyes of a dead, heavy hawk
until she said, "Time for lunch."
                It was on the little hill,
in the plicae of scions and immortelles,
they ate rice and cream,
stared into the shadows
and napped, quite snug,
by the hawk beneath
the little dove tree.

HER OWN

In this room, she has drawn butterflies
on sheaves of cream and phthalo paper,
arranged chromatically by color,
so the right-winged blue-blue, left-winged near-blue-blue
is just right of the right-winged near-blue-blue,
left-winged near-blue-blue, and so on.
On the north wall are red, orange and yellow;
on the east, green and blue; on the south,
indigo and violet.
   Some wings are clipped, some Klimt
patterns with ebony eyespots are quadrupled
near the rims of the wings, symmetrical
arches of harps, arch and doorways of chitin.
   In this room, there is no one to tell her
that time cannot be felt. She feels there is, there
must be, another way to measure
time: not in minutes but in thoughts, time's
very texture, or at least the texture
of her perception. If she could, however
gradually, increase her number
of thoughts per minute, and then per second,
she could elongate what she knew. In this room,
there's no one
to tell her differently.

www.ingramcontent.com/pod-product-compliance
Lightning Source LLC
Chambersburg PA
CBHW031609110426
42742CB00037B/1504